GROTTO HEAVEN

Jonathan Stalling

Chax Press
Tucson 2010

ISBN 978 0925904 92 8

Printed in Canada by Friesens

Published by:
Chax Press
411 N 7th Ave Ste 103
Tucson, AZ 85705-8388
USA

洞天

石江山／著

茶客寺 出版社 (Chax Press)

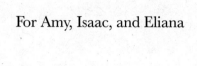

For Amy, Isaac, and Eliana

Introduction

Sequence One: *The Practical Chinese Reader* is a rewritten chapter
of the ubiquitous Chinese language textbook produced by Beijing
Foreign Language University: *Practical Chinese Reader* (PCR) that I first
studied Chinese from as an adolescent and teenager. Here, I re-imag-
ine the text as the space of a heterolingual encounter where one can
attend to the presence of a non-acquired language without seeking to
master it. Attending, which denotes a careful bending forward with-
out necessarily apprehending what one attends, replaces acquisition
as the aim of study. Such an attention does not seek to domesticate
the unknown, or make the world beyond my language into acces-
sible knowledge. This chapter offers an alternative to mastery as the
measure of learning and imagines a relationship with the otherside
of one's language still in the darkness of its absolute obscurity.

Sequence Two: *Grotto Heaven* 洞天 continues to pursue the possibility
of attending the foreign in a heterocultural imaginary (woven from
Daoist tropes and subterranean Ozark landscapes) where the body is
transfigured into an aperture through which readers may enter into
a non-allergenic relationship with darkness (like that of unknown
languages) without recourse to the metaphysics of translation (the
oldest faith-based initiative). In the poems of *Grotto Heaven*, the body
become a cavern (洞, cave, itself a synonym for inquiry), which in
turn becomes a sinkhole into the night sky, where spelunkers can tra-
verse the bureaucracy of stars to attend to the still, pregnant cloud of
dark languages before becoming (our) syntax. Here in the continual
embryo, space is constantly born and pushes outward harder than
gravity pulls us back in. And we are a part of the outrushing, where
light (interpretive clarity/certitude) is an anomaly best viewed within
its oceanic context.

Known languages are not so different from light: they enable one to construct or imagine totalities, but are only a small fraction of the 7,000 human languages that appear as darkness to any one of us at all times. *Grotto Heaven* attends to that which doesn't appear (as vision) by bending forward without recoil or demand for light (translation). How to see without light, how to be with the outside of one's languages? How, in short, can one attend to the dark still in its darkness? The first two sequences offer a space before the orientation known languages provide, where poems are but tipping points forward.

Sequence Three: *Lodge* ·· 宿 departs from the theme of relating to the unknown by way of leaning toward it, past a return to a unified, knowing self by acknowledging the already plural relations at "home." Here the term *lodge* is explored as another measure of attending to relations already always within the self's space. As a noun *lodge* is a small usually temporary dwelling, (a tent, arbor, hotel or the like); it is a place of sojourn, a place to accommodate, or a collection of objects "lodged" or situated close to each other. In this sense, I want to explore the self as such a constellation or aggregate, of tightly packed relations lodged in temporary shelters. As a verb the term denotes extending hospitality, receiving others into one's home, providing habitation, harbor or seeking shelter in or from another. Such a verb is less an action taken than an action already taken. Becoming aware of this, however, is awakening to dependence, and in that sense, the ethics of being. The first two sequences deploy a mysticism that moves away from the traditional desire for an identity with divinity and the certainty, knowledge, vision, and power such an identity would mobilize. But here (in the third sequence) one no longer needs to leave for relations to emerge. Lodged, we appear in the half-light, as multiple, shifting configuration of relations with(in) others. In Chinese, lodge 宿 is both the verb "to lodge" for the night

8

(xiǔ), a lodge (as in hotel) and the ancient word for a celestial con-
stellation (xiù): The poems in this sequence explore this contingent
withness of this being.

The Compiler
Buffalo, NY 2001-2005
Norman, OK 2005-2009

I⊙

Practical Chinese Reader:

A Revised Grammar Book

目　錄
(Contents)

弟 七十二課　　Lesson 72

前言　　　　Introduction..7

一，課文　　Text..14

二，生詞　　New Terms...17

三，注釋　　Explanatory Notes (冥: Darkening Into the Perceived)..19

四，替換与擴展 Expand through substitution drills...............................21

五，語法　　Language Laws..23

　　　　　　一。外國語是什麼？ (What is Foreign Language?)
　　　　　　二。赴; 照顧 (Attendance)
　　　　　　三。聽寫 (Dictation)
　　　　　　四。口音; 問候 (Greeting; Accent.)

八，跋文　　(Epilogue)...26

九，漢字筆順 Character Practice..28

洞天　　　　Grotto Heaven 29

星圖　　　　Star Charts...51

宿。。　　　Lodge 57

13

弟 七十二课
Lesson Seventy Two:
课文
Text
弗认兰谷围哲
Foreign Language

说明: 这是一首用中文写成的英文诗, 当朗读它时, 英语国家的
听众听到的是英语, 而中国听众听见的是中文。你将发现诗歌存
在于两种语言之间的黑暗地带。

Explanation: The English poem below is written in Chinese, so when
it is read aloud, the English speaker will hear an English poem, while a
Chinese speaker will hear/read a Chinese poem, the poetry lies in the
darkness between.

闭上眼睛
    Close your eyes
   kē lù zī yóu 'ér 'āisī
       珂露姿犹而哀思,
       Jade dew appears as mournful memories

    一个幽暗的房间
      In a dark room
     yǐng 'è dá 'ér kè rú mù
        影厄答而克如木,
        Narrow shadows controlled answer as a forest

睁开眼

       Open your eyes
    'ōu běn yóu 'ér 'ǎi sì
        欧本犹而霭寺,
        Gulls' origin is a mist-enveloped temple

再睁开眼

       Open your eyes again
    'òu pén yǒurì 'āisī 'è gǎn
        怄溢有日哀思厄感,
        Frustration overflows a day's grief
           as a narrow sensation

幽暗的房间外面

       Outside the dark room
    'āo tè sāi dé dì dá 'ér kè rùmù
        凹特塞德地答而刻入暮,
        Concave particulars are better than
           virtue, earth replies by carving
           toward half light

有一张脸,将你凝视

       A face watches you
    'è fēi sī wò chísī yòu,
        厄飞思卧驰思幼,
        Distressed, flying laying down
           pining for childhood

凝视黑暗
Watching the dark
wò chí yǐng dì dǎ rì ké
卧驰影地打日殻
resting on flying thoughts
earth beats upon
the sun's shell

(New Words)

珂	kē	◊ jade-like stone
露	lù	◊ dew, drink distilled from flowers, reveal, in the open, out of doors
姿	zī	◊ looks, appears
犹	yóu	◊ just as, still, even
而	'ér	◊{grammar}...and...but...to...at...when...if...
哀思	'āisī	◊ mournful thoughts, of the lost, grief
影	yǐng	◊ shadow, image, a trace, a sign, a reflection, a play of shadows
厄	'è	◊ a narrow pass
答	dá	◊ responds, returns
克	'ér	◊ able to
如	rú	◊ compare with
木	mù	◊ a tree
欧	'ōu	◊ Europe, or "ßu": vomit
本	běn	◊ root, stems, origin,
靄	'ǎi	◊ mist
寺	sì	◊ temple
恼	'òu	◊ annoyances
溢	pén	◊ gush forth
有日	yǒurì	◊ for days
感	gǎn	◊ feel, perceive, as if sensitive (to light)
凹	'āo	◊ concave, sunken, hollow
特	tè	◊ only
塞	sāi	◊ fills in

德	dé	◊ virtues, mind, kindness
地	dì	◊ the earth, land, and soil
刻	kè	◊ engraves, carves, the moment
入暮	rùmù	◊ towards evening, at nightfall, at dusk, half-light
飞	fēi	◊ of birds, flying, hovering, soaring
思	sī	◊ thinking, desiring
卧	wò	◊ to lie down, to recline
驰思	chísī	◊ to remember an absent person
幼	yòu	◊ a young, child, to nurture
驰	chí	◊ rush, spread out, crave, desire
打	dǎ	◊ beat, break, smash,
日	rì	◊ the suns
壳	ké	◊ shell, housing, surface

注釋 (explanatory note)
冥: Darkening Into the Perceived

一。　　Even after

　　　　　　the night

　　　　　　　　　gown of beaded

　　　　　　　　　　　and rushing away stars

　　　watching

　　　　　　on the comfortable curve

　　　　　　　　of eyes

　　　　　　　　　　tracing the arc of anything

　　　　　　　　　　　　mind stumbles into

二。　　　　Wide,

　　　　　　　　the sky

　　　　　　　　　　　falls　forward

　　　　　　in spite　　of　　the hair

　　　　　　　　and wave

　　　　　　　of distant　　bright

　　　points

三。

In darkness

　　the

　　　　　desire for light's kind　　of knowing

　　　　　pulls hard　　through the pupil's gate

So close　　them

　　　Whole　and
Enter

替换与擴展
"Expand, through substitution drills."

一。 Light is not _____ but _____ we see.

a star	a far
a distance	a mesa
an opening	thought
an escape	language
an entrance	below

二。 Darkness is not _____ but _____ we see.

what	how
disclosed	displaced
bound	shuttered
traversed	a threshold
there	where

三。 What appears as _____ from _____ slips away.

a star	a far
a distance	a mesa
an opening	thought
an escape	language
an entrance	below

四。 _____ pushes harder than _____pulls.

Anything	nothing
Nothing	anything

語法　Language Laws

一。　外國語是什麼？
What is Foreign Language?

The category of foreignness　　does not refer here to languages,

but a relation　　to their

power to mean

without yielding to the subject's

mind.

Mastery,　forgets

the weight　　of the Foreign,

that its obscure　　mass and energy

will always　　dictate the outrushing

of the universe

二。 Attendance 赴; 照顧

　　一。　　Attending the foreign

　　　　　　releases　knowing as the measure

　　　　　　　　of relations.

　　　　unabled by darkness
　　　　　　　　　　emerge there as its acquaintance

三。 Dictation 聽寫

　　一。　　To speak the foreign　　　　without deciphering

　　　　　　　　is to lean toward,　　　momentarily,

　　　　past a return.

　　　　　　　　It is to hear voices in darkness

　　　　　　　　　　and vanish into the greeting.

24

四。 Greeting; Accent: 問候; 口音

一 。 The student's accent exceeds its container
revealing a voice that overflows language and body
to become the very measure of attendance

        the brushing
        up against,

        of script, lips, teeth, tongue,

the air pushed across the alveolar ridge,

blushes.

    kē lù zī yóu 'ér 'āisī

    珂露姿犹而哀思

and enter

八，跋文
(Epilogue)

Foreign language
外国的语言

                cannot be settled.
                无法定居。

the darkness   of its distance
                  is   its principal   measure.
距离的黑暗   是   它唯一的尺度。

                for
                因为

Foreigness is not subject
    陌生的东西   to discovery
                      不能发现

                          cannot be dis-covered.
                          无法揭开。
Its cover   is not a language
    表面的语言
                  I can learn   or peel away.
                  我不能学会   无法剥离。

                yet
                然而

        Learning does not have to be a discovery
        学习不必成为发现

It is not after all a frontier

它毕竟不是征战

        Please let it not be a frontier.

        请不要让它成为征战。

九，漢字筆順 Character Practice

弗									
认									

兰									
谷									

围									
哲									

II⊙

洞天

Grotto Heaven

內練習　　　Inner Exercises

一。

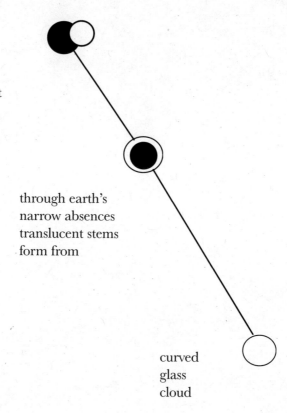

Now stand
sassafras root
spills down

through earth's
narrow absences
translucent stems
form from

curved
glass
cloud

Shift weight

from heel
to toe

from a
gray lake

the reflection
of your spine
urges up

across the back

waves cut
and overturn

in respiration

a pheasant   opens   iridescent   fan   as   if   oil

32

三。

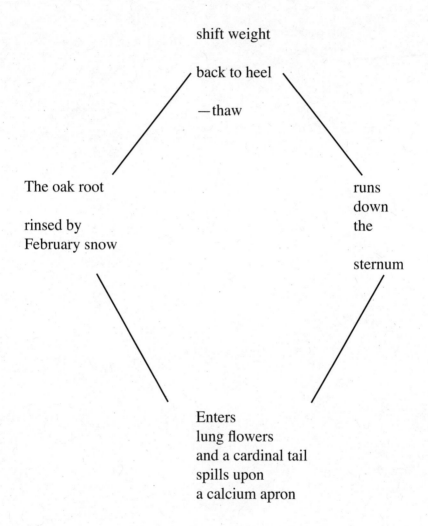

shift weight

back to heel

—thaw

The oak root

rinsed by
February snow

runs
down
the

sternum

Enters
lung flowers
and a cardinal tail
spills upon
a calcium apron

四。

shift weight
to left foot,
hands rest
at side

The pond
at the base
of the skull

joins slope
of shore
shawl and
clay

a king fisher
perfectly still
eyes dream stems
lit at the ends

五。

Shift

weight   ◯   to right

foot

hands

turn   ◐   upward

Cross

creek

of   ◉   cotton

wood
plume

六。

nocturne

birds ⊙ untie

the suture

weight

doesn't ◉ return

to center

cloud

stem ○ s and

pearl

做凹山, Constructing a Hollow Mountain

Take a piece of paper,

fold it into a cone

tight at the top

and wide at the bottom

                              draw cliff and hollow,

                              oak and dogwood

                              texture from underbrush to
                              bough

Imagine the world above

the convex cone

of mountain slope

and boulder for

the ocean of stars are

the mountain's context

now release the paper,

let it resume its natural shape

pick it up and fold the cone again,

this time outside in.

Diminish to an ounce,

& enter the concave mountain

star lumen falls from

deep beneath the earth

where they flicker

through soluble veins

now

enter again

this time

from behind the lids.

洞天　Grotto Heaven

一 。來到　Arriving

rust　　riverbed roads　　line with trees　　of dried sunfish
----------------------\　　\--------------------------------------
eyeless fish　　swim　　　　　down darkless　　　　　tunnels

a truck kicks red　　　　　dust up　　against　　　　the banks
--------------------\　　　　\--------------------------------------
flowstone　　　　smoothes down　　to vein's origin

a farm houses　a man who　bends　　space around　his children's　eyes
------------------------\　　\--
seeds drip　　from stone straws and　　grow in,　　if not　　a rhythm,
imagination

the spring　　pools outside　　perfectly　　clear and cold
-----------------------\　　　\--
speleothem-abras　　　　spill　　　from flowstone

eyes　　claim space　　as if from　　origin
--------------------\　　　\--
pupils bloom　　nocturnal to swallow　　your eyes whole

二。 入門 elementary/entrance

Eye vanished　　　behind　　the outer gate

half pools　　below

thoughts' yielding,

toward　　the draught,

vanish　　　　　cloudlike or of　ice

flowstone　　smoothes down to　　inlet

limestone yields　　through　the pupil

because

because　provides　　ample cause

　　　　　　　　to climb down.

三。 傾斜 Slope

The instant　　provides　　an aperture,

release breath　　and enter　　beneath its ceiling,

watch footing,　　twist　　into walls till　　root

from rural　　nocturne　　to the calcite gate

melted stone warped　and beveled　till karsk scape

scatters　　with sharp stones

　　twenty feet　to slope

and fall　　toward water.

darting lights

　　squint beams,　　waver, click

四。玄 Dark

Turn off the lamps

Even hands are on the otherside

close your eyes behind the retina

now open   and open again

darkness is not   a phenomena

or place

not what   but how we see

五。魚 Fish

Beneath the hidden mirror   of the lake

pale fish, skin of milk,

       a film and circulatory iron

skin over   eyes leaves

     different tunnels
           open

dark doesn't land   upon   things

    isn't a   thing   after all

break dawn's   focus and   flow   in

    spill in   another measure.

darkness just isn't there.

六 。洞時 Cave Time

The cave,   stone vein

slope   and   wail

is   the breakdown,

of   light,

soluble stone

yields in   its phase   before

cave   flowers   wax

from the   same,

counts   time

in drape   and push

helicite hair   not incandescent

but

stay here
                unheard of

45

七。 韻腔 Hollow Tune

Karsk forms

                                 other entrances

collects from bloom   and attention

as trochee

cave seeds   drip

                     from   stone stems

and throw   a single   if half strong   echo

stress   unstress,   stress,   unstress

karren   and   cavern

cone and crevice

if not a rhythm   imagination of measure

the echo of pulse or fall

八。內洞 Inner Cavern

Suture   sinkhole

from the other   side   up

                open

to or as

day threads   from a spool of   light

        quite through   the pupil   then   pulls

gently   till taut

as form   and desire

know   and falls

to shed   his steps

九。 服光 Gathering Lumen

like waves

the kind   certain words
spark

between the roots   and their   inflec-
tions.

The hole

offers not perception,   but closer

and fear spills down

through the dislocation   of thought
and

stone

if by parallel opens into the half

light of syntax,

a calcite fabric too fragile

to be

constellations

✝。 ..

the final room

isn't the final   room

but   the sky   in all directions

this gate is not cut

                    but fell here and will keep

shifting till settled
                        into collapsed entire

                        space is   no more   than

                        the   direction   we face

                        the pathway   or veins

                        meander up now

                        to star extensions and flow

                        up to their eyelet's break and fall

星圖

Star Charts

一。 東方青龍

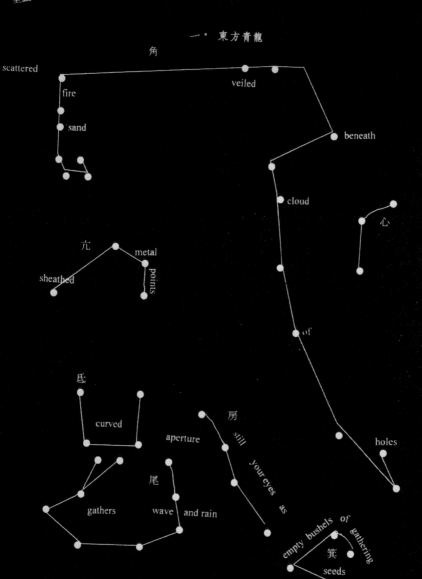

53

北方玄武

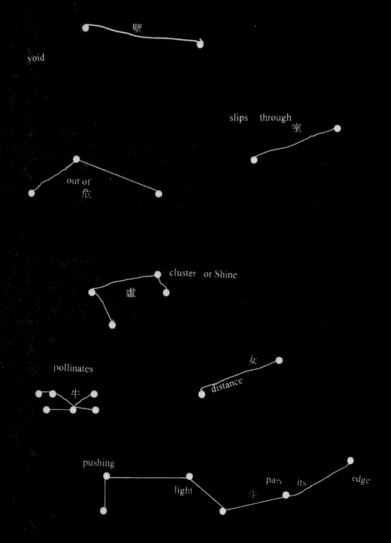

void

slips   through
室

out of
危

cluster   or Shine
虛

女
pollinates
distance
牛

pushing
past   its   edge
light
斗

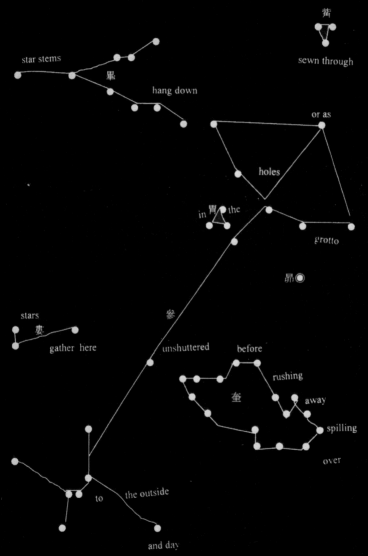

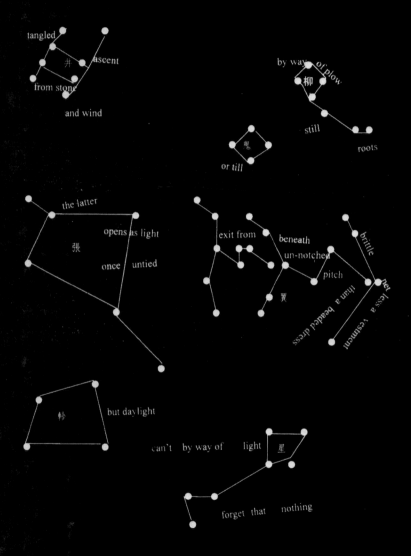

南方朱雀

tangled

井 ascent

from stone

and wind

by way of plow

柳

still

roots

鬼

or till

the latter

張 opens as light

once untied

exit from beneath

un-notched

翼 pitch

brittle

net

than a beaded dress

less a vestment

轸 but daylight

can't by way of light 星

forget that nothing

pushes harder than anything pulls.

III⊙

Lodge

.

.

宿

Even in our act of pointing

it seems we are a we
before trying to be

outside
of us
or in a space
to leave from

Supplanted

Here among us
the I is an outflow

The experience of staring
mirrored
in the glassweave

less bound
to the wavefall of light
than shifting rudderless
than ambiguously edged
than stubbornly expressed waves
formed in the act of falling

Diffuse,

I am then as much
as now the with
between us

encircle the lodge before entering
encircle the circle afterwards

Outside
children from another prefecture
disrupt the narrow lanes
halfway around the world
they are more than a dream of our context
and you are more than the dream of mine

The Space
(for amy)

Opened by your voice
cannot be reduced to body
or language yet the I
that takes place here
isn't one without it

The movement and event
of the sounding itself
is the lodge
the taking place of us
appears here in the encounter
which opens as our own

A self is a rupture in awareness
housing windows
bridging the echo's return
and forgetting the mirror's immensity
polishing cannot vanish
the obscure approach

Becoming the chamber
of a self isn't a place or presence
just the name of returning to or from
the sound of your voice

love

sounds
like a kind of   distance
is spelled   like   a kind of distance
means
in most cases
                  what   distance means
When flown into
                  becoming
                        the space of us

The River Wear
shaping Durham's seven hills

    Tilting toward us
    are cloisters
    of clinging opaque sun

A cloth dream of Cuthbert's shrine
Northumbria in late sleep
or in my mind

    Pieces of an eve and the milk
    inside you from all sides
    wasn't light or blizzard

But imagined gathering
about your form
as of candles
tilted at the unknown
as an invitation to become more

                County Durham—Northumbria

Back in Edinburgh,

The wind falls dark by 3:30
we try to gather ourselves
but the stones are soaked through

      you are a valley of oak
      outflowing the forms

      of the mind folded in
on the idea of more
a falling down upon
a swift unsayable cradle

                  Edinburgh

With the New Year

gorse returns a field
of glass stones

Scattering earth lamps on Arthur's Seat
awashed
in shining out stories
aflamed through

Shown as a field of slipping
or falling sound

from *haly ruid*

Wherefrom miles away
you have crossed the sea.

Edinburgh

Time

    slips through

the caesura--

    as a

loose reaching toward

another sound

                            Atlantic

Rajorshi's insistence

that loss predominates
that the waves were everything
and that the ocean

A figment or memory of her hair
as if enunciating her name would
canvas the rain pooling in the roads

tied
nearly audible
Isaac threads us
through the Atlantic mirror

Edinburgh—Munster

A ripple in the words

Or an opening beneath them
is small enough
for children to take place

To overtake communication
the rupture itself
becomes the very heart of the world

The countless garden is the ease
of loving them

Munster—Buffalo

small

legs
running

a continuum
of wing
wobbling
light

What a thing!
we don't have children

Anymore than the atmosphere

Buffalo—Norman

Celestial

leaf
his eyes are more than I can handle
his laughing is an outside of my own mind
emerging continual rupture

> only one thing more frightening
> than listening to the stammer
> murmuring
> small silvery insects
> in their chests
> cellophane wings
> almost light

what does it mean?
no shore
or cusp
to them
less a shelter
than
everything
open to chance

Norman

In the half dark

Eliana is pure current
>Her voice exceeds the language it carries
>and spills over us as

>Ecstatic blue flame
>to become the whole of what it means
>to be spoken to

Nearing syntax
>we are made of her language

>I can't wait to pour cereal
>into her chipped green bowl

Norman

We need not gather each other

into the cotton sieve
of a gentler interpretation
or wrap this withness
into a tissue of unvoiced fricatives

        we are not quietly decidable
        sound or noise
        we are barely the possibility of
        consonants

but we come to these languages
and the vapor leaking from them
to vanish
into our relations
within relations becoming
each other's

        swift
        unsayable
        candles

                           Norman

lodge

.

.

宿

众友们，我等皆天宿星，共宿一宿矣，明日天亮即散。

(Friends, we are constellations for a night
then disappear in the light)

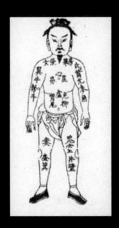

About the Author

Jonathan Stalling lives with his family in Norman, Oklahoma, where he teaches Poetry and Transpacific Literature at the University of Oklahoma. He is also the author of *Poetics of Emptiness: Transformations of Asian Thought in American Poetry* (Fordham University Press, 2010), and an editor of *Chinese Literature Today* magazine and book series.

About Chax Press

Chax Press was founded in 1984 by Charles Alexander as a creator of handmade fine arts editions of literature, often with an inventive and playful sense of how the book arts might interact with innovative writing. Beginning in 1990 the press started to publish works in trade paperback editions, such as the book you hold. We currently occupy studio space, shared with the painter Cynthia Miller, in the Small Planet Bakery building at the north side of downtown Tucson, Arizona. Recent and forthcoming books by Alice Notley, Barbara Henning, Charles Bernstein, Anne Waldman, Tenney Nathanson, Linh Dinh, Mark Weiss, Will Alexander, and many more, may be found on our web site at *http://chax.org*.

Chax Press projects are supported by the Tucson Pima Arts Council, by the Arizona Commission on the Arts (with funding from the State of Arizona and the National Endowment for the Arts), by The Southwestern Foundation, and by many individual donors who keep us at work at the edges of contemporary literature through their generosity, friendship, and good spirits.

This book is set in John Baskerville's eponymous typeface in 11 point size with other sizes used for titling, as well as a variety of Chinese language fonts. Composition and design in Adobe InDesign.